I Thought I Loved Me Too

Carolina Olivas Flores

BookLeaf Publishing

India | USA | UK

Dedication

To anyone who needed to be saved but didn't think to save themselves.

Preface

This book is a compilation of poems I've written throughout the years, from as early as my teen years up until my mid 20s. I always struggled with choosing myself, choosing who to love, when to walk away and how to set boundaries. I can't tell you that it gets easier, in reality it gets harder and harder and then one day it gets easier but then you repeat the cycle and it gets harder than ever all over again. But this life we live is full of love. Every tragedy can be a lesson, it can be a story to share, the love that breaks us doesn't stop being love. If this book finds you I hope it makes you feel less lonely, that no matter what happens before or after a heartbreak you will find love again, some days you will find it within you, some days in others, be open to love as many times as it comes knocking at your door, but most importantly don't forget that its all about you and how you love and forgive yourself countless times.

I've always loved listening to music as I read so here is a playlist to go along with the book:

1. Big Jet Plane by Angus and Julia Stone
2. The Night We Met by Lord Huron
3. honeymoon blues by bast
4. Pluto Projector by Rex Orange County
5. Comedown by Joesef
6. affection by BETWEEN FRIENDS
7. Plastic by Moses Sumney
8. Remember Me by UMI
9. 8 by Billie Eilish
10. Feeling Whitney by Post Malone
11. Wake Up Alone by Amy Winehouse
12. worldstar money (interlude) by Joji
13. Sparks by Coldplay
14. Cherry Hill by Russ
15. MINE by awfultune
16. lvr boy by awfultune
17. Paper Thin by Lianne La Havas
18. If I Get High by Nothing But Thieves
19. If You're Going To Break Yourself by Unknown Mortal Orchestra
20. Teeth (Interlude) by XXXTENTACION
21. Strange by Celeste

22. Mice by Billie Marten
23. Mr.Sun (miss da sun) by Greentea Peng

Acknowledgements

I'd like to thank Myself for taking a step forward in writing my first official poetry book. We often always forget to love or put ourselves first, so for once I'd like to give myself my own flowers.

Black Rose

During this season I am not the prettiest
nor the brightest rose in the garden
I am the deadliest
the one whose petals are now turning black
and are now falling one by one to the ground
where soon the wind will carry me away and kiss the
rest of me goodbye

I am not looked down at, nor appreciated
but as the winter ends and spring comes
I flourish once more
I slowly bloom
and my petals are now as red as the blood on your finger
tips
from which my thorns have clinched onto you after
trying to pick me off the ground

I only wish to be admired for my natural beauty
leave me in my natural habitat
where you can water me and admire me
even come near me just to sniff my petals

for which if you were to pull me out
with time I would only slowly die

and this time when winter is now gone
and spring is back in town
it will be too late
I would now have turned black
and I would never bloom once more

you might have me for you to keep for a while
but once I am dead
you will simply toss me out and go out for more
I do not belong in a tall vase
filled with your sink water
I do not belong in a room where I am alone
I belong home
in *my* home
Do you understand?

I might die once in a while at home
but I never stop flourishing and coming back to life once
more.

Don't gamble with life

If you don't choose who you love, life will pick for you and life can be cruel.

Ruins

The homes that I've built have holes in the walls
the floors creak with every step you take
the roof is constantly leaking
and the water over pours with waste

the homes that I've built have ghosts that haunt me day
and night
the lights are always flickering
the hallways are long and narrow
and its impossible to walk through them
they feel endless
you can hear echos with no response

the homes that I've built are cold and lack insulation
yet no one can hear the screams that are coming from
the inside

the homes that I've built are inexpensive but have cost
me everything
they are always occupied with the same people
the gardens never bloom
and the grass is always greener on the other side

the homes that Ive built have never felt like home
and yet I've resided in them for years.

I don't love you

I know I shouldn't be thinking about you
I feed myself with lust and day dreams
but you fit in my mind so well
youre the perfect villain to either break me or grow with
me

To be human...

I think I'm a pretty decent human being
Im fairly honest
I try to love all, even the bad
I try not to judge, especially myself
I can be alone and not feel lonely

But sometimes I do lie, specially to myself
I also get impatient with the people I love
and I allow others to use me when I do feel lonely
so I might not even be that decent, just human.

sink or swim

I want to *think* that everything is going to be okay
but i *feel* like everything is going to come crashing down
as hard as I'm working to keep a float, I still feel like I'm
drowning
I feel suffocated
I feel stuck
and I'm trying so hard to keep swimming
but the tide just keeps dragging me back down
I try to float
I try to gasp for air
but the pressure keeps me down.

Journey

We all get lost on the way
its okay to pick up rocks as you walk the trail
drop one, step by step
it will help you find your way back
thats if you want to go back where you left of on
if not, there's a whole world out there waiting to
discover *you*
go look for yourself and you'll find what it means to be
alive.

Home is where you are

I always wanted it to be you
in my head you were everything, even when you gave
me nothing
I was always so quick to rush to you when you'd call
no matter the time or place, I'd be there
you'd say *come* and Id run there
you'd say *speak* and I'd bark
you'd leave and I'd follow
I would've followed you anywhere
even to my own destruction if it meant I'd get to be by
your side
but you never picked me
you never chose me
you never even considered me
and still, I always will want it to be you.

There is no maybes

Maybe today I'm just too depressed to do anything
maybe its the gloomy weather that makes me feel like
this
maybe if I just stop listening to sad music I will stop
thinking like this
maybe if I knew how to make better choices I wouldn't
be here
maybe one day I will have it all figured out
maybe tomorrow I will have it all together
maybe
just maybe...
just
listen...
I know I will just be back here tomorrow telling you the
same old story.

Potential

I wish you were better for me. I always run back to you
thinking this time will be better.

I taste you on my tongue and the bitter taste of your
mouth makes me realize that you don't taste as good as I
always fantasize. Thinking *this time it'll be different* and
it always ends up worse than the last. I can't shake this
feeling off, I can't stop running back to you any time you
call. I refuse to accept reality, but then I have you face to
face once again and the disappointment settles in. *How
did I end up back here again?* Knowing the exact
outcome but choosing to believe this time would be
different. I couldn't see you for you, for all that you'd
show me. I lived with the idea of you. I wanted to believe
that my perception of you was caring. But you only
cared to know you had me at your disposal, seeing how
quick I'd jump to the sight of you. My mind played tricks
and I'd fall for them... I'd fall for you. Over and over and
over. I wanted to believe in a fantasy I had made up of
my own.

I am your favorite poem

I am a poet
and its hard to understand myself
I try to wake up at five in the morning every day but I
always end up waking up at noon
Im an artist, I love to mix and match colors and patterns
I always leave a mess no matter how much I pick up and
clean
I change my mind every second and decide to change my
jacket over and over again
next thing you know there's a pile of thoughts left
all the possibilities my mind creates coexist
I love the night time
when the rest of the world is asleep and I'm walking
around like its my playground and I own it
I dance as I walk and others stare
I sing as they talk and they wonder what goes on in my
head
I am loud and wish to be softer sometimes
but I am who I choose to be
and it may be messy
or crazy
or even eccentric
but its what makes me happy
its chaotic most of the time but i wont fight to change it

anymore
I am change
I contradict every choice and action I make
I am a paradox
I change with the seasons as the seasons change with
time
Im not the expected change
I just wake up and choose to be whatever makes me
whole
I can be poetry
I can be art
I can be your favorite lullaby
I can be everything and nothing all in one.

From me, to the version that needs to hear it the most

I wish I could tell you that we make better choices now
theres days we do but then we fall back into old patterns
and repeat the cycle
but its okay because we no longer look at life like a
punishment when "bad" things happen to us
we accept it, we understand there's a lesson to be taught
in all that we experience
and within everyone we meet, we don't look at anyone
or anything as "evil"
we understand they all have their own demons and its
not our fault how anyone reacts or treats us
the only responsibility we have are our own emotions,
our own truth, our own choices
we don't blame ourselves, we nurture ourselves and try
to be compassionate when we make mistakes
this life wasn't made to be perfect, it was made for us to
create our own reality
one where we take our own hand and say "it's okay to
start over as many times as you need to"
because life doesn't end when we can't break the cycle, it
ends the moment we give up
so you try and you keep on trying the best that you can
without ever being afraid of failure

because if you're reading this, you're still here and you
made it this far
even after all that has happened, we are still here.

Nyctophile

I can be as dark as the night in a New Moon phase
where the only thing that shines are the stars
I may or may not be appreciated
I may be perceived differently
some may be afraid of the total darkness
but if ever lost you can follow the constellations to find
your way back

In my nights of Full Moon I am the brightest
I am the most loved, seen and appreciated
I walk with you and follow you around wherever you go
with a full moon you never feel alone in the night

When the Crescent moon appears I turn into art
I am the most admired
I am the most mysterious
and everyone watches me in awe

As for the remaining phases of the moon
I am forgotten
I am under appreciated
no one bats an eye
everyone awaits for these phases to pass
they are not exciting nor interesting nor beautiful

they are just a pass time until the better phases appear

as you can see, I am only loved conditionally
I am not for everyone
but I am one with the night
no matter which phase appears
the night covers me into its arms
It appreciates my change, my many phases and both my
dark and bright days
it knows my cycles and understands that I can change
from one day to another
its the night that never leaves my sight

Too blind to see

You know for someone who loves *love*, I find it funny
how I've always struggled to love myself
I always saw so much beauty in everything but never
within me
It takes so much out of me to be compassionate with
myself over others
I could tell someone all the steps to love themselves but I
never applied those steps into my life
and that's okay because I am the love I give to others,
even if I can't see it sometimes.

Poison

I can't find any excuses to not tell you how much I love you, so I drink to find one instead.

?

I've lived a happy life for the most, yet pain is the only
thing that's ever made me feel alive.

Secret Garden

Stop lying to yourself
you put your wall up so high
no one could climb it
theres a whole world on the other side
youre to afraid you'll be rejected
or that you'll be hurt again
but life and time passes by
and I would hate to see you waste it by being bitter
don't be afraid to love again
love is all we have

Far far away

If you knew me you would know how much I hate you
but since you don't, you truly think I love you
All the pain you've cause me just passes right through
you
you may think I stay because this is what you think I
want
but I stay because I see no escape
you always find a way to keep me
but I just want to escape
I want to be as far away as possible from you
I want to live in a world of my own
where only I belong

Dear Mr Sun

I know I should come out to see you more often
I forget how good you can be for my mental health
lately that's all I've been needing, just a little light
like all flowers, I too need sunshine to grow
on gloomy days I miss your warm hugs
and with a little rain you add colors to the world
reminding me that even on the darkest days there's still
a reason to shine bright
even when no one can see you, your presence is always
there
so if you can choose to show up for me every day
I too can show up for myself

<3

I love all
I love even those who have hurt me
I love those who have shown no respect
I love those who I once "hated"
I love all because I know what its like to feel invisible
I know the feeling of irrelevance
I love because even if that love is never reciprocated, I
know that I still loved unconditionally

I crave to be loved
not used or lusted
I want to choose
I don't want to be picked
picked flowers die out
you can only keep them in water for so long
I want to be the flower in your garden
the one you go out to water every morning as the sun
rises
I want to be truly admired
not possessed

www.ingramcontent.com/pod-product-compliance
Lightning Source LLC
La Vergne TN
LVHW021807210726
843510LV00018B/1673